TRUSTWORTHY AND TRUE

Barbara Ann Kleck

WORD & SPIRIT
PUBLISHING

Scripture quotations marked NIV2001 are taken from the WOMEN OF FAITH STUDY BIBLE Zondervan

Trustworthy and True
Copyright © 2025 by Barbara Ann Kleck
ISBN: 978-1-685730-78-9

Published by Word and Spirit Publishing
P.O. Box 701403
Tulsa, Oklahoma 74170
wordandspiritpublishing.com

Printed in the United States of America. All rights reserved under International Copyright Law. Content and/or cover may not be reproduced in whole or in part in any form without the expressed written consent of the Publisher.

Dedication

This book has been written *to honor* the Holy Trinity—Father, Son, and Holy Spirit—as trustworthy and true, so beautifully described in Isaiah 9:6: "Wonderful Counselor, Mighty God, Everlasting Father, Prince of Peace."

It is *dedicated to* the many people who—throughout my lifetime—have influenced, encouraged, and even challenged my faith in Jesus Christ. Many of those beautiful souls now reside with Jesus in His heavenly realm, I am sure. I am especially thankful for and grateful to members of my earthly family and my extended family of brothers and sisters in Christ.

It is *written for* anyone who desires encouragement to begin a relationship of trust in God, or for those who could benefit from encouragement to deepen the relationship of trust already established. It is my sincere belief that by also reading the Bible passages to which I refer, the greatest benefit will be realized by the reader.

Sincere thanks to the people in my life who have encouraged and supported me to publish this book, including the fine people of WORD AND SPIRIT PUBLISHING. Without you all, these pages would have simply remained a little puff in the sky where many dreams die.

A Word of Encouragement

Sometimes when I sit down for my time of meditation in God's Word, it can feel like I am only going through the motions. Though my eyes are focused upon the page and the words I read, I am only minimally present. My heart and mind seem to be elsewhere.

If you experience times like this, I encourage you to stick with it: persevere, pray, and continue reading. Keep in mind that many things outside of you are vying for your attention, even working diligently to distract you from obtaining the peace, joy and encouragement that our heavenly Father wants to offer you through His Holy Word and your time with Him. Eventually I am sure you will experience what I have experienced many times: with the combination of your own perseverance and God's Holy Spirit working within you, you will connect and engage in a beautiful experience of meditation.

Holy Father, it is so good to know and to trust that even in the times when I am not "with" You, You are with me; drawing me in and loving me through Your sweet Holy Spirit! Amen.

He leads me beside quiet waters, he restores my soul. He guides me in paths of righteousness for his name's sake.

—Psalm 23:2–3

Note: Righteousness is not something I can accomplish in myself…by doing the right things or being a certain way. It is all about who God is and what God does in a person who accepts Jesus Christ as Lord and Savior. I love the definition in the dictionary of my Bible: "Righteousness is the fulfillment of the demands of a relationship. God brings believers into a right relationship with him, erasing their guilt and crediting righteousness to them (Romans 3:21-22) and helping them to be devoted to the service of what God says is right (Romans 6:11-13). Page 2102 WOMEN OF FAITH STUDY BIBLE

Introduction

Webster's Dictionary defines *trust* as "reliance on the integrity, veracity of a person."

My simple meaning looks like this: Trust is confidence in the honesty and truthfulness of another.

As a young child, I had mostly positive experiences with trust. I was fortunate to have parents, grandparents, and siblings who were trustworthy. But as my world expanded into the outer community, I began to understand that not everyone deserved my trust. And the older I became, the more I found this to be true. As all humans, I learned to trust people through my own experiences. I learned *not* to trust people in the same way.

Some scholars are very sure that people who have trust issues with others will also have trust issues with God. Though that may have been true for me for a period of time, it is no longer true. God has proven to me, time and again, that He is faithful. He is not fickle, tricky, or fallible. He is trustworthy and true. And it is through my daily decision to trust Him that He continues to show me that He can be trusted.

I hold to the thought that trust is a word of action, which means that I move toward God and His ways and away from things that would hinder that forward movement. With this mindset, I am made ready to boldly and confidently trust.

If you know me personally, you know that my life has been very messy in many ways. But thanks be to God, I have seen some wonderful changes that continue to take place as I trust in His redemptive work upon my life. As I have heard others say, I agree: the story of my life is God's story, too.

It is my hope that you, the reader, will find encouragement for your own journey in trusting God through what you read of mine. Most important, I hope that you will allow God to speak personally to you through His Holy Word. Jot down your thoughts in this book or in your Bible to make and keep a personal journal of your own walk in faith.

If you do not have a Holy Bible that you can hold in your hands and write notes in, I encourage you to purchase one. There are many versions from which to choose. Start with one that appeals to your own desire for additional support (such as maps, dictionary, concordance, etc.) and that is written in a style that is easy for you to read and reference.

1

Father, Son, and Spirit—Three   Yet one God:
　　　　　　　　　　　　　　　　true, Holy Thee!

God of old and God of new: Creator, Savior, Spirit, too.

Changeless throughout time remain, and all of life
　You do sustain.

Forgiveness is Your greatest bliss:
　Your Holy Word speaks much of this.

How ever could I *not* adore The God You are forevermore!

　　　With all my heart, I praise You, O God!

Trust in the LORD *with all your heart and lean not on your own understanding; in all your ways acknowledge him, and he will make your paths straight. Do not be wise in your own eyes; fear the* LORD *and shun evil. This will bring health to your body and nourishment to your bones.*

　　　　　　　　—Proverbs 3:5–8 (my life verses)

See also: Psalms 89:14–17; 103; John 3:16–17; 10:22–30; Hebrews 1:1–12. Read the amazing story of God's first recorded workweek in Genesis 1 and 2:1–3.

2

Some people seem very puzzled when I say that God speaks to me. Perhaps they even believe I am a little crazy. But this I know: He speaks—loud and clear.

> I hear You in the morning. Your voice is loud and clear.
> As I read Your Holy Word, in love You draw me near.
>
> I hear You in the midday when the sun is bright.
>
> I can't mistake Creator God in fragrance, sound and sight.
>
> And as the sun is setting, I hear Your calming tone
>
> within and all around me . . . I know I'm not alone.
>
> One more thing discovered: at any time of day
>
> You're never, ever nearer than when I bow to pray.
>
> With all my heart, I adore You—
> the God who speaks in so many wonderful ways!

Praise the LORD, *O my soul; all my inmost being, praise his holy name. . . . For as high as the heavens are above the earth, so great is his love for those who fear him; as far as the east is from the west, so far has he removed our transgressions from us.*

—Psalm 103:1, 11–12

See also: Psalms 19; 119:89–93; 139:1–18; 145; John 10:14–15; 2 Timothy 1:13–14; Hebrews 3:7–10; Revelation 3:19–22.

3

God's Word promises that He is present everywhere, at all times, and in all circumstances of this life.

I praise and thank You, Father for Your Holy Word divine,
handed down through all the ages even into hands of mine.

Words of old, yet rich in story do intrigue and magnify
Your deity and compassion and how You reign on high.

Not as tyrant do You govern, but as loving Father, You
are watching, guiding, leading those whose hearts are true.

You've despised man's stubborn waywardness as still You do today,
yet in mercy sent the Savior to guide hearts back Your way.

With all I am, I thank You for Your Word, such treasure key
that somehow through the ages travelled all the way to me.

> With all my heart, I adore You—eternal, holy Father!

The grass withers and the flowers fall, but the word of our God stands forever.

—Isaiah 40:8

See also: 2 Samuel 22:31; Psalms 119:89–91; 105; Isaiah 55:8–11; John 1:1–4;14; James 1:22–25; 2 Peter 1.

4

Life is full of contrasts: blessings and challenges; joys and sorrows; sweet moments and sour ones; light and dark; good and bad; abundance and poverty. Opposites abound. Yet in and through it all, God is faithful to those who call upon His name.

Though at times this world is hard, I'm blessed with peace
   and hope.

By trusting You in all I see, it's possible to cope.

You know the pathways I must walk because
   You've walked them, too.

You've felt the fear of death and dark, but You walked
   right on through.

It gives me peace to know that I am never all alone.

Surrounded by Your love and power, I'm seen, and I am known.

   With all my heart, I adore You - God who sees me!

I sought the LORD, and he answered me; he delivered me from all my fears.

—Psalm 34:4

See also: Psalms 27:1–3; 91:1–2; 117; Isaiah 41:10; Hebrews 2:9–18.

5

Every single moment of my life has been, is now, and always will be in God's hands. Nothing passes into or out of my life without His knowledge. Though I make choices all day, every day, of what to do, I am confident that God is watching over me, caring for and loving me through every moment of every hour.

> Beautiful Risen One, Prince of my heart,
> I treasure the thought that You never will part.
>
> You'll be with me always, as always have been.
>
> When life takes me down, You'll raise me again.
>
> From the very beginning You've been my true friend,
> my Alpha, Omega, beginning to end.
>
> With all that I am and ever will be,
> I give thanks and praise for Your love for me.
>
> With all my heart, I adore You—
> the One who knows and cares for me with everlasting love!

O LORD, you have searched me and you know me. You know when I sit and when I rise; you perceive my thoughts from afar. You discern my going out and my lying down; you are familiar with all my ways.

—Psalm 139:1–3

See also: Psalm 89:1–2; 2 Corinthians 4:16–18; Philippians 4:4–9; Revelation 22:13.

6

Every day of my life, I make thousands of little choices that feed into the next choice. As they accumulate, those choices paint a picture that I view at the end of the day. Will I like what I see in that picture?

When it's time to arise, will I choose to remain cozy and covered until the very last possible moment and then rush into my day? Or will I allow myself the luxury of time to awaken in a peaceful way, even spend some time with my Lord in prayer and meditation? What will I choose to put into my body as fuel throughout the day? Will it nourish me in healthy ways? If I interact with others, how will I choose to do so? Will their days be blessed because our paths crossed? The choices I make regarding what to look at and listen to will impact my thoughts. Will those choices add peace and joy or bring anxiety and shame to my thoughts? What will I choose to wear? Will it be a good reflection of how I wish to be seen? Where will I go? How will I go? Will those choices promote wholeness and safety? Will I choose to be patient and kind to those I encounter in my travels? In which conversations will I engage, and from which ones will I disengage? If what I am doing is stressful, will I allow myself time to break away, breathe, decompress, and show kindness and honor to my body and my mind? With whom and what will I choose to engage in my free time? Are my choices healthy and life-giving for both myself and those I love? Do my words and actions at any given moment in my day reflect the "me" I want others to know? How do I speak to myself and others when mistakes are made? Do my words reflect grace? When the time comes to lay my head on the pillow to rest, do I choose thoughts that will promote relaxation and peaceful slumber? The list of choices is long. The one who chooses is me.

So many choices in one little day. What will I do? What will I say?

How will I live to honor my life even if there is heartache
and strife?

One choice is made; then comes the next. Will I be joyful,
or will I be vexed?

So much to consider as choices are made. And it all goes much
better if I have prayed.

> *Choose my instruction instead of silver, knowledge rather than choice gold, for wisdom is more precious that rubies, and nothing you desire can compare with her.*
>
> —Proverbs 8:10–11

See also: Psalm 86:2–7; Proverbs 16:6–7; Matthew 5:43–44; 6:5–15; Philippians 4:6–9.

I have lived in and through disappointments and heartaches of many kinds. And in the midst of those things, I have made some decisions that have impacted others and myself in big ways. Though I prayed for guidance, contemplated outcomes, and sought guidance and counsel from people I trusted, it is clear to see in the lookback that some of the decisions I made were not good. And this I have learned: no matter how much time, effort, and prayer I put into my decision-making, there will be consequences of some kind that must also be lived through. But if I take responsibility for the consequences as well as the decisions, I can find peace and joy as I continue to trust in God to lead and guide me forward.

Decisions I made long ago have impact on today.

If I knew then what I know now, would I have chosen other way?

I could not see the future; I did not have a clue.

I only knew the way to go was to put my trust in You.

And so, I trusted as I prayed though many tears did fall,
and in my heart I knew for sure that You were watching all.

I can't go back. Old days are gone. But this much I do know:

By trusting You in my today, You'll help me live and grow.

    With all my heart, I adore You—sweet Redeemer!

Trust in him at all times, O people; pour out your hearts to him, for God is our refuge.

—Psalm 62:8

See also: Psalms 40:5; 139:23–24; Hebrews 4:14–16.

8

I struggle from time to time with getting out of my own history. Though my past is certainly done and gone, it can easily creep back into my awareness. Memories of poor choices and blatant sinfulness that I have already confessed still rise up to condemn me in the present. I know where this comes from: condemnation does not come from the Lord. And so in the moments of temptation to regress, it is up to me to rise up, claim my victory, and call upon my Savior to go to battle on my behalf. Each time I do, He does.

> I love Your sweet surprises, Lord, though sometimes I am blind
>
> by concentrating on the things that I have left behind:
>
> the losses and the heartaches; the disappointments, too.
>
> While focusing upon what's past I'm missing what is new.
>
> Sweet Savior, in such moments, raise my mind to see
>
> the time now passing: here and now is the best place I can be.
>
> > With all my heart, I adore You—
> > precious Warrior, dearest Friend!

Therefore, there is now no condemnation for those who are in Christ Jesus, because through Christ Jesus the law of the Spirit of life set me free from the law of sin and death. For what the law was powerless to do in that it was weakened by the sinful nature, God did by sending his own Son in the likeness of sinful man to be a sin offering.

—Romans 8:1–3

See also: Isaiah 50:7–9; John 3:16–17; 2 Corinthians 5:17; Ephesians 4:22–24; Colossians 2:6–8.

9

Though my tendency may be to run from pain and problems, I have found that when I simply calm myself down and trust God, I can walk through anything. Blessings show up in the problems; joy eventually wraps itself around sorrows. God's grace gives me courage, peace, and hope, even in the most unlikely circumstances.

Even in my darkest hour, You are here with grace and power,

reminding me of whose I am: a child of Yours,
the Shepherd's lamb.

By trusting You, peace comes to me

as I walk through adversity.

With all my heart, I adore You—Good Shepherd!

*The L*ORD *is my shepherd, I shall not be in want. He makes me lie down in green pastures, he leads me beside quiet waters, he restores my soul. He guides me in paths of righteousness for his name's sake.*

—Psalm 23:1–3

See also: Matthew 11:28–30; John 10:14–15; 15:5–8; 2 Corinthians 1:3–4.

10

Many times in my life, I have been deeply hurt by others through things that were spoken or done to my loved ones or myself. Not being a good fighter, I have swallowed many very angry words that I really wanted to say. Instead, I hauled the garbage of grudges around inside of me ... until I started to understand what that garbage was doing to me and to my healthy relationships.

I have a better plan now, though it sometimes takes a while to put it in motion. I quickly forgive and pray for those who cause me pain. That doesn't mean I forget what was done or said, but it moves me into a better place in my head. And I trust God to handle all the details, knowing He loves both of us: the one who offended and me.

Holy Father, here I come; I'm bruised and very sad
to tell You what You clearly see: someone has made me mad!
There's really nothing I can do; my hands are clenched up tight.
And I am feeling energized to start a great big fight.
I know it is not wise for me to carry on this way.
The other person's Your child, too. So I will stop and pray.
Calm this storm inside of me. Tear it all apart.
Change my focus—but most of all, calm my raging heart.
Bring Your peace to this big mess. Remind me; help me see
a better day is coming soon by simply trusting Thee.

> With all my heart, I adore You—
> the One who sees, accepts, and helps me as I am!

Man's anger does not bring about the righteous life that God desires. Therefore, get rid of all moral filth and the evil that is so prevalent and humbly accept the word planted in you, which can save you.

—James 1:20–21

See also: Psalm 139:23–24; Proverbs 14:21; 15:1; 29:11; Matthew 6:12–15; 18:21–35; Ephesians 4:29–32; Colossians 3:13–14.

11

There are times when, after someone has asked for my forgiveness or I have asked it of someone else, I am left with a lingering feeling of unforgiveness that just will not go away. In these times, I must be diligent in prayer regarding my own issues. Sooner or later, the truth of my unforgiveness will come into my awareness. And it's usually not pleasant to acknowledge. Nonetheless, it is important to pursue and correct if ever I hope to move forward in forgiveness.

> I just can't seem to drop this thing! It clings to me like glue!
> So in this moment, here I am, surrendering it to You.
> Please take this unforgiveness, Lord, and all that strings along.
> I bring it, Jesus, to Your cross. I'm weak, but You are strong.
> I'm weary and I'm tired, Lord; worn out in many ways
> from hauling all this garbage around so many days.
> I seek release and freedom. I ask You: help me see
> what is it that needs to change within this heart of me?
>
> With all my heart, I adore You—the One who sees my heart!

Search me, O God and know my heart; test me and know my anxious thoughts. See if there is any offensive way in me, and lead me in the way everlasting.
—Psalm 139:23–24

See also: Psalm 51; John 3:16–17; ; Ephesians 6:14–15.

12

God's presence in my life transports me through the toughest of times. And though I may not see His movements, it becomes very clear that He is with me when I simply trust that He is.

> You go with me. You walk beside
>
> no matter where I go.
>
> In Your presence I'm at peace.
>
> Your love for me You show.
>
> Whether bright or darkened skies,
>
> I never have to fret,
>
> for there's no place—no height, no depth—
>
> where You have not been yet.
>
> With all my heart, I adore You—God with me!

You will keep in perfect peace him whose mind is steadfast, because he trusts in you.
—Isaiah 26:3

There is no pit so deep that God's love is not deeper still.
—Corrie Ten Boom, holocaust survivor

See also: Psalm 89:15–17; Isaiah 40:28–31; Romans 8:38–39.

13

I trust God to watch over those I love. He is good. His love and His mercies have no end. Throughout time, from one generation to the next, God has shown Himself faithful to all those who call upon Him.

> All those I love I bring to You,
>
> for You are good; Your Words are true.
>
> And I know they'll no safer be
>
> than in Your care and loved by Thee.
>
> With all my heart, I adore You—
> the One who watches over my loved ones!

Those who know your name will trust in you, for you, Lord, have never forsaken those who seek you.

—Psalm 9:10

See also: Matthew 19:13–14; Philippians 4:6–7; 1 Peter 5:6–7.

In my moments of intense fear or concern regarding my loved ones, I love to use Psalm 139 as my prayer. Instead of reading it in first person, I exchange all I – me – and my with the name of the person for whom I am praying – along with inserting the correct pronouns to complete the prayer.

14

Because of God's great love for me, I am learning to trust more and worry less about my own life and the lives of my loved ones.

> Through hope and trust I find You near,
>
> confident that You are here,
>
> standing with me every hour,
>
> giving peace and showing power.
>
> Even in the biggest mess,
>
> with all I am I can profess,
>
> You are Lord of life to me . . .
>
> The one true God—all praise to Thee!
>
> With all my heart, I adore You—
> the One who is always and everywhere!

"Who of you by worrying can add a single hour to his life?"
—Matthew 6:27

Never be afraid to trust an unknown future to a known God.
—Author Unknown

See also: Psalm 105:1–4; Isaiah 9:6; John 14:15–17.

15

How great is the love and faithfulness of God! Through all the pages and ages of time, He has shown His powerful and unwavering love to mankind—even in the midst of man's sinfulness and calamity. It brings comfort and hope to me to know and to trust that to the end of all time, no matter what may come, God is and will be the same God to me that He was to those who lived in the very beginning of time.

> Make of my life a sacrifice,
>
> complete in trusting You.
>
> And let no shame make me lame,
>
> but keep me steadfast, true.
>
> So in this life and through all strife,
>
> I'll simply trust Your love
>
> that shines down bright through darkest night
>
> from Your dear throne above.

With all my heart, I adore You—Creator God of mercy and love!

> *Praise the* LORD. *Give thanks to the* LORD, *for he is good; his love endures forever.*
>
> —Psalm 106:1

See also: Matthew 5:14–16; John 8:12; 1 Peter 2:9.

16

It is possible to say that I trust God—but actually doubt Him—if I hold Him to my own understanding of possibilities. I can declare that I trust Him for healing and at the same time doubt His ability to heal because I cannot imagine how He could do it. That is not trust. It is just lip service. And I am pretty sure that God is not amused by it.

> Help me, Lord, remove myself as I trust in You
>
> for things I can't imagine that You could ever do.
>
> Your powers are beyond me; I'll never understand.
>
> Your ways are so much higher than hills in any land.
>
> Forgive me, Father, when I doubt or deny Your ways.
>
> You have shown me many times there are limits to my gaze.

With all my heart, I adore You—God beyond my understanding!

> *"For my thoughts are not your thoughts, neither are your ways my ways," declares the LORD. "As the heavens are higher than the earth, so are my ways higher than your ways and my thoughts than your thoughts."*
>
> —Isaiah 55:8–9

See also: Psalm 25:8–10; Isaiah 40:28–31; Matthew 21:18–22; Mark 11:20–24; Romans 8:38–39; 11:33–36; James 1:5–8; Jude 18–22.

17

I trust Jesus to be my very best Friend. But sometimes, I need an earthly friend whom I can see, touch, and speak to—and who responds to me.

Sometimes I need to laugh or cry with a human who laughs and cries; who actually sits across the table, shares a secret, rolls the eyes, and reminds me that in this world I am not alone. I am among other human beings who struggle with doubts and fears, who share oxygen and the earth with me right now.

Earthly friends who love You, Lord are of my greatest treasures.
Their worth to me I cannot count. It goes beyond all measures.
In them, I find real hopefulness when I am feeling blue.
Through them, I get encouragement I'm sure comes straight from You.
I thank and praise You, Father, for human friendship's love.
It's living, breathing proof to me You see me from above.

With all my heart, I adore You—
Giver of every good and perfect gift!

Every good and perfect gift is from above, coming down from the Father of the heavenly lights, who does not change like shifting shadows.

—James 1:17

See also: Proverbs 17:17; 18:24; 24:24–25; 27:5–6; Ecclesiastes 4:9–10; John 15:9–17.

18

Perseverance is essential for many things in life, whether those things are pleasant to do or unpleasant.

The dictionary ties the word *persist* to *persevere.* The thesaurus adds words: *continuance, steadiness, tenacity, pluck, stamina, bulldog courage, resolve, stick-to-itiveness,* and *endurance.*

In the words of Oswald Chambers: "Perseverance is more than endurance. It is endurance combined with absolute assurance and certainty that what we are looking for is going to happen."[1]

You make what seems impossible quite possible for me.

I'm aware it's not my own power or energy

that keeps me hopeful when I'm sad and helps me persevere.

It's not me, but You, dear Lord, and all the ways You're near.

I praise You for the ways You work to help me on my way.

It gives such peace and joy to me to know You're in each day!

With all my heart, I adore You—God who perseveres through me!

> *His divine power has given us everything we need for life and godliness through our knowledge of him who called us by his own glory and goodness.*
>
> —2 Peter 1:3

See also: Psalm 46; Romans 5:1–5; Philippians 4:6–9; Hebrews 12:1–3; James 1:2–4.

19

For many years, I struggled to understand myself, others, and the world through the ways of the world—only to discover that a worldly understanding will never bring truth. It is as elusive as a gnat in a fruit bowl: real and plainly in sight one moment; invisible in the next.

Only trusting in God and His Word for answers and understanding can bring peace to my soul. And so that is where I choose to spend my energy.

> There will always be positive and negative,
> > the good and the bad,
>
> the light and the darkness, the joyful, the sad,
>
> the wealth and the poverty, the push and the pull,
>
> the peace and the chaos, the bright and the dull,
>
> the hopeful and hopeless, the quiet, the bold,
>
> the near and the distant, the new and the old.
>
> In the mix of all things that are and will be
>
> I choose to live life by trusting in Thee.
>
> > With all my heart, I adore You—
> > my Source of all hope and peace!

How sweet are your words to my taste, sweeter than honey to my mouth! I gain understanding from your precepts; therefore I hate every wrong path. Your word is a lamp to my feet and a light for my path.

—Psalm 119:103–105

See also: Proverbs 3: 5-8; 17:27–28; Ecclesiastes 3:1–8;
1 Thessalonians 5:16–18.

20

When I am in distress, I call out to God, and I know that He hears me. Forever He is faithful; forever He is near. He is my hope, my anchor, my rock, and my peace. He is the One upon whom I rely. There is no help for me in all of the world that is greater than His steadfast, trustworthy love.

> Far beyond all mortal love,
>
> You reign as Father—high above.
>
> You show You love me very much
>
> through earthly trials, troubles, and such.
>
> Just as my father's arms were strong
>
> and sheltered me from world gone wrong,
>
> Your love surrounds me night and day
>
> to give me courage on my way.

With all my heart, I adore You—divine heavenly Father!

You are my hiding place; you will protect me from trouble and surround me with songs of deliverance.
—Psalm 32:7

See also: Psalms 28:7–8; 46; 143:8; John 16:33; 1 Corinthians 1:25; Philippians 4:13.

21

I am aware that if I choose to refuse to see God, the likelihood of seeing Him is very, very slim. So I have decided to live my life fully alive and aware of God's presence because I want to see Him—and I trust that He is with me in every breath and every step. I believe that He sees the path that is at my feet as well as the pathway that is yet beyond my vision. And before I arrive at one journey's ending place, I believe that He is ready and waiting to lead, guide, and help me on to the next.

> I've come to realize, day by day
>
> that sooner or later, most things won't stay:
>
> people will move; the storm will move on;
>
> the flood will subside; there'll be a new song;
>
> the taste won't remain; the memory will fade;
>
> I will feel different about the price I have paid.
>
> But one thing I've seen will surely remain:
>
> Your love and Your faithfulness through all my pain.
>
> With all my heart, I adore You—the One who travels with me through all difficulties and dilemmas!

This is the day the Lord has made; let us rejoice and be glad in it.
—Psalm 118:24

See also: Psalms 36:5–9; 90:1–2; 93:1–2; Isaiah 26:4; 64:4; Lamentations 3:19–23.

22

What will keep God from loving me? Will it be my sinfulness? My stubborn nature? My anger or my jealousies? My disappointments in this life? Is it any physical distance I try to create between myself and Him? Or a barrier I construct in my mind? Is it any calamity or disaster? Is it where I live—or where I am going?

Nothing at all can or will keep God from loving me.

Doubts sneak in the back door.

That's just what they do,

enticing me to wander

and look away from You.

But hold me: keep me steady,

no matter what may be.

Remind me that You love me.

And hold my gaze to Thee.

With all my heart, I adore You—
the One who loves me through all my doubt!

For God so loved the world that he gave his one and only Son, that whoever believes in him shall not perish but have eternal life. For God did not send his Son into the world to condemn the world, but to save the world through him.

—John 3:16–17

See also: Psalms 18:1–3; 34:17–19; 71:1–6; 139:7–18; Acts 17:24–28; Hebrews 11; 12:1–3.

23

I have dedicated my life to following Jesus. I believe that He is always with me: watching over, guarding, guiding, protecting, and loving me as the divine Savior and Good Shepherd He is. No matter how I may be feeling or what I am going through—whether I follow Him energetically or half-heartedly—I know that His love pursues me throughout time and eternity.

As You lived and moved so long ago, You live and move today…

perhaps not in a physical form, but in Your own sweet way.

In compassion You appear when things are going wrong

to raise the gate; to bring Your light; to give my heart a song.

Though worldly cares will always be, it brings my heart delight

to know and trust Your Spirit moves to bless with peace and might.

With all my heart, I adore You—beautiful Holy Spirit of God!

For this God is our God for ever and ever; he will be our guide even to the end.

—Psalm 48:14

See also: Psalms 24; 89:5–8; 136; 147:5; John 14:15–27; Revelation 1:8.

24

Sometimes when I am facing a time of anxiety, and I open my eyes to another day, I wonder: What will happen next . . . and after that? It can be hard to imagine getting through the day. On those days, it is my faith and trust in God that propels me with courage to toss back the covers, put my feet on the floor, and get going.

When I am troubled and full of care,

it helps me just to trust You're there

to guide and point me in the way

to just live out this one short day.

No other guide for me will do:

I know I'm fully known by You.

> With all my heart, I adore You—
> the One who knows me . . . guides me . . . loves me!

I will praise you, O L<small>ORD</small>, among the nations; I will sing of you among the peoples. For great is your love, higher than the heavens; your faithfulness reaches to the skies.

—Psalm 108:3–4

See also: Psalms 25:4–6; 27:13; 61:1–2; Proverbs 4:11–15; Isaiah 40:10–11; 1 John 3:1.

25

As a small child, I had a dream of becoming a professional ice skater who could dance and jump and twirl on shiny skates, while wearing cute and sparkly skating outfits. Watching such skaters on TV inspired my dream. And it looked so easy! When I told Mom about my plans, she simply said, "That will take a lot of practice."

Fast-forward a few years to the ice rink in my community; a shallow pond in the park managed by the local fire department. With my borrowed skates laced up tight, I wobble-walked onto the ice. Down I went. Up again. And down again. My fear of falling a third time in front of my friends led me back to the bench from which I'd come. My hope of ever becoming a professional ice skater melted away right there. Clearly, that particular dream was *not* for me.

Dreams of childhood flew away as quick as they flew in.

Looking back is comical. It even brings a grin.

You had other plans for me, designed by Your own hand.

And if I'd hone the gifts You gave, I could someday land

upon the joy of talent that You give to all so free.

And there would be no need to strive for dreams not meant for me.

With all my heart, I adore You—God of all blessings...
the One who knows my future!

*Many, O L*ORD *my God, are the wonders you have done. The things you planned for us no one can recount to you.*

—Psalm 40:5

See also: Psalms 42:5; 139:12–16; Isaiah 40:28–31.

26

When things are not going well, I can feel lost in this world—wandering about in my mind as if I have no future, no hope. But in the very moment that I remember it is God who holds all my days, I come back into the realities of the moment with joy and thanksgiving. God is my hope for today. And He is already in my future.

> There is blessing in seeking and trusting You
>
> in what to do.
>
> There, I'm free as I can be.
>
> No chain of doubt to tangle me,
>
> no trap, no snare, no worldly care—
>
> just confidence that You are there.

With all my heart, I adore You—beautiful Prince of peace!

Who shall separate us from the love of Christ? Shall trouble or hardship or persecution or famine or nakedness or danger or sword? As it is written: "For your sake we face death all day long; we are considered as sheep to be slaughtered." No, in all these things we are more than conquerors through him who loved us.

—Romans 8:35–37

See also: Psalms 23; 37:39–40; 147:7–11; Proverbs 3:5-8

27

In all things and through all things, God is with me—whether I am aware of His presence or not. His ways do not depend upon my knowing. Even when I am at my worst, He is with me to console, comfort, and bring about changes within and around me for His glory and my good.

It is Your strength and not my own that walks me through each day.

Joy or sorrow on my path, Your Spirit guides my way.

Not one moment of any hour do You leave me alone.

But in Your mercy, grace, and power, You love me from
    Your throne.

What comfort, peace, and joy it brings to know You care for me!

You know my name . . . You see my life. Through who You are
    I'm free.

With all my heart, I adore You—always-present Father and Friend!

> *You hem me in—behind and before; you have laid your hand upon me. Such knowledge is too wonderful for me, too lofty for me to attain.*
>
>   —Psalm 139:5–6

See also: Romans 8:18; 2 Corinthians 5:7; 1 John 1:5–7.

28

Many times, I have become impatient for changes in my life or in the lives of others. I've wanted things to happen *now*. I've wanted others to see things *my* way—as if I knew best, as if I had the ability to see into the future. But then, a quiet moment of revelation comes in: only God knows and can see the whole picture—even how the present extends into the future. And I am reminded it's better if I just get out of the way and give whatever it is to God.

> Moment by moment and day after day,
>
> You invite; You inspire; You show the way
>
> to trust in Your mercy, Your love, and Your power
>
> as I live out my life from hour to hour,
>
> teaching me patience to wait on Your will,
>
> to honor Your ways, and to let worries be still.

*I am still confident of this: I will see the goodness of the L*ORD *in the land of the living. Wait for the L*ORD*; be strong and take heart and wait for the L*ORD*.*

—Psalm 27:13–14

See also: Psalms 40:1–3; 130:5–6; Isaiah 30:15–18; Matthew 6:31–34.

29

When challenges come along, I can be confident to face them—not because of my own abilities or knowledge, but because I know God and I trust Him to help me. I have seen His love and care in action throughout my lifetime—sometimes in the energy and talents of others I know, and even in and through strangers who seem to come along at just the right time. God is good—always good. I can and will trust in Him.

> What a difference in my day
>
> when I trust in You along my way!
>
> Troubles come—they always will—
>
> and it helps to pray before each hill.
>
> Somehow, it's then an easier climb.
>
> Somehow, You move ahead of time.
>
> Somehow, You grant me hope and peace
>
> Somehow, Your mercies do not cease.
>
> With all my heart, I adore You—the One who has proven to be so very worthy of my trust!

I guide you in the way of wisdom and lead you along straight paths. When you walk, your steps will not be hampered; when you run, you will not stumble.

—Proverbs 4:11–12

See also: Psalm 9:9; Philippians 4:4–9; 1 Peter 5:8–11.

30

As God's child, I know I can come to His throne of grace in prayer at any time. I lay my requests at His feet in confidence and trust that He will regard each one—but give me only what is good for my life.

> Every detail of me You know:
>
> where I've been and where I'll go;
>
> when I rise and where I'll fall;
>
> You see and care about it all.
>
> Especially in each troubling hour,
>
> there You are with grace and power
>
> to help me raise my weary head
>
> and turn from hopelessness and dread.

With all my heart, I adore You—gracious and loving Father!

Be joyful always; pray continually; give thanks in all circumstances, for this is God's will for you in Christ Jesus.
—1 Thessalonians 5:16–18

See also: Jeremiah 17:7–8; Matthew 6:5–13; Mark 11:25; Romans 8:22–27.

31

Waiting for God to answer prayer can be difficult—even agonizing—until I remember that it is God—the Creator, the King of the universe—upon whom I am waiting. Who am I to think I can push Him, or His timing, to answer me?! So . . . if I become willing to change my focus from my agenda to *who God is*, the time of waiting can become a beautiful adventure—a mystery. Moments become more meaningful. And sometimes, my agonies can even become exquisite opportunities to grow and change.

> In my times of waiting,
>
> if I remember that You care,
>
> that You're watching, guiding, loving,
>
> no matter when or where...
>
> if I remember that Your faithfulness
>
> reaches far beyond my years,
>
> my heart will fill with hopefulness,
>
> and I can stand above my fears.
>
> With all my heart, I adore You—
> the One who hears every prayer!

The Lord your God is with you, he is mighty to save. He will take great delight in you, he will quiet you with his love, he will rejoice over you with singing.

—Zephaniah 3:17

See also: Psalms 27:13–14; 139:1–18; Proverbs 16:9; ; Matthew 7:7–12; Hebrews 11:1–2; 12:1–3.

32

Traveling through this life and into new experiences can sometimes feel like a walk on a balance beam that has been raised too high for me. My head tells me that I could fall and fail miserably at any moment. But my heart knows that if I do, God will be there with His strong arms of mercy ready to embrace me. And in that knowledge, I am able to continue.

> When the storms of life are raging
>
> and the waves come crashing 'round,
>
> while my boat is rocking wildly. . .
>
> Your presence is my ground.

With all my heart, I adore You—awesome Prince of peace!

The eternal God is your refuge, and underneath are the everlasting arms.

—Deuteronomy 33:27

See also: Psalms 9:9; 62:5–6; Romans 15:13.

33

When I view my situation and the problems I can see before me, and I think only of my own resources and strength, I may become overwhelmed. But if I look at the situation through the light of God's love for me, hopefulness comes in: I can see possibilities, I feel loved, and I am able to carry on—even joyfully.

> Not through flood like Noah faced, but floods of other kinds,
> You have helped me, Father; You have calmed my mind.
> You have granted wisdom and courage for each task
> as I focused on You and in faith did ask
> for help to tread the waters that all around did rise.
> In those troubling moments I could feel Your eyes
> watching, loving, guiding, and giving me a hand
> as I moved through my rough waters until I reached dry land.

With all my heart, I adore You—the One who helps me through troubles of this life—even the ones I create for myself!

Surely God is my help; the Lord is the one who sustains me.
—Psalm 54:4

See also: Psalms 18:30–34; 42:11; 46; Hebrews 13:20–21. Also, read the amazing story of God's grace shown to Noah and his family in Genesis 6 through 9.

34

No matter how I may try to rearrange what I know, see, and hear, sometimes this life is not fair. Very bad things happen to very good people, and people who do very bad things get away without even a reprimand. Though I may be able to make no sense of things, I have found that if I will trust God, I may eventually see His hand at work in even the worst situations.

> If I expect this life to be always good and fair,
>
> I'll be disappointed, and I'll be full of care.
>
> This life can be confusing. It cannot always be
>
> what I hope or pray for or what I'd like to see.
>
> But if I trust Your wisdom, Your compassion and Your way,
>
> I can be hopeful, looking forward to each and every day.
>
> With all my heart, I adore You—the One who knows the beginning, middle, and end of all things—good and bad!

The LORD works righteousness and justice for all the oppressed. He made known his ways to Moses, his deeds to the people of Israel; the LORD is compassionate and gracious, slow to anger, abounding in love. He will not always accuse, nor will he harbor his anger forever.

—Psalm 103:6–9

See also: Psalms 23:4; 97:10; Proverbs 24:19–20; Isaiah 5:20–21; Romans 2:8–9; 5:1–5; 12:9, 17; Ephesians 1:3–10; 1 Peter 3:8–12.

35

If I keep my mind and my heart open along the way in any day, I will find evidence of God's presence. He is already ahead of me and has placed many blessings along the pathway—more than I will ever be able to recognize or comprehend.

I'll go out in gratefulness to live this little day.

I'll trust in You to walk with me and guide me on my way.

Though troubles come, as sure they will, I'll walk a steady pace

while counting on Your help and love, Your guidance and
    Your grace.

Just one short day in history is knocking at my door.

I'll live the day with all I am and hope for many more.

> *Praise be to the God and Father of our Lord Jesus Christ! In his great mercy he has given us new birth into a living hope through the resurrection of Jesus Christ from the dead, and into an inheritance that can never perish, spoil or fade—kept in heaven for you.*
>
> —1 Peter 1:3–4

See also: Psalms 34:8; 86:5; 118:24; 119:169–176; Matthew 22:34–40; Galatians 5:16–18; 1 Peter 2:1-3

36

There are times when every sight and sound around me invites me to fear. But when I choose to refuse to be led by fear, and I place my hope and trust in God instead, I am empowered to be courageous and confident.

> Though fears may come in every size
> to knock upon my door,
> when I put faith ahead of me,
> I see Your love galore.
> For in the shadow of Your love,
> I'm safe, and I am free.
> No earthly trouble of any size
> needs to bother me.
>
> With all my heart, I adore You—
> the One who is greater than all my fears!

He will cover you with his feathers, and under his wings you will find refuge; his faithfulness will be your shield and rampart. You will not fear the terror of night, nor the arrow that flies by day, nor the pestilence that stalks in the darkness, nor the plague that destroys at midday.

—Psalm 91:4–6

See also: Proverbs 29:25; Luke 12:4–7; Ephesians 6:10–18; 1 John 4:13–18.

37

I get really frustrated with myself sometimes. It seems I have to learn God's truths over and over again to finally "get" them. I may simply be a person who learns slow. But I am certainly thankful that my Teacher is the patient, compassionate, forgiving, and redeeming kind!

Why would I choose to hold a grudge when I could set it free?

The one who actually loses the most is really, truly me.

Why would I cuddle and hold it tight as if it were a prize?

It's just a ploy of darkness wrapped up in disguise -

making me think I'm powerful, and I have got the edge -

when the simple truth is, I'm its slave, hiding behind a hedge!

> With all my heart, I adore You—the One who patiently teaches me to see my foolish ways!

As God's chosen people, holy and dearly loved, clothe yourselves with compassion, kindness, humility, gentleness and patience. Bear with each other and forgive whatever grievances you may have with one another. Forgive as the Lord forgave you. And over all these virtues put on love, which binds them all together in perfect unity.

—Colossians 3:12–14

See also: Psalm 139:23–24; Matthew 5:43–48; 6:12–14; 7:1–5; 18:21–35; Luke 6:31–36.

38

God's Word is abundant in stories of His love and faithfulness, told through the lives of people in Bible times who honored, loved, and trusted Him. In their presence, God showed Himself to be kind, loving, and full of mercies. He performed miracles and wonders that stretched beyond human understanding.

The same Holy Word is loaded with stories of how God is tough; He means what He says, as was made evident in the lives of those who doubted or deliberately turned from His ways.

I can benefit in my life by learning from the lives of all of these people if I am willing to allow their experiences to speak to me.

It's not mine to understand Your complicated ways,

but just to trust—to hope—to pray—and fix my human gaze

upon the path that I am on and in Your strength to rest,

while knowing in my heart and mind Your plan is always best.

So, as You ask, I'll do my best to live by trusting You.

And in my heart, I'll hold the thought: Your love for me
 is true.

> With all my heart, I adore You—
> everlasting, faithful God!

For the word of God is living and active. Sharper than any double-edged sword, it penetrates even to dividing soul and spirit, joints and marrow; it judges the thoughts and attitudes of the heart.

—Hebrews 4:12

See also: Genesis 22:1–19; Luke 1:3–25, 57–65; Hebrews 11; 12:1–2; 2 Thessalonians 2:16–17; 1 John 3:1.

39

In the presence of evil, it is normal and appropriate for me to feel fear because I clearly understand that satan and his ways are bigger and stronger than me. But they are miniscule in comparison to God, His power, and His love. And so, if I concentrate upon my faith and trust, I can be calm and rest assured that He is with me . . . even in the presence of fear.

> In the light of Your presence,
>
> there's hope, and there's peace.
>
> Darkness won't win,
>
> and grace will not cease.
>
> Time and again
>
> You've proven to me,
>
> You are my stronghold:
>
> God who makes me free.

With all my heart, I adore You—the One who guides, guards, and protects me from evil!

Submit yourselves, then, to God. Resist the devil, and he will flee from you. Come near to God and he will come near to you.
—James 4:7–8

See also: Matthew 13:24–30, 36–43; Luke 4:1–12; Ephesians 4:26–27; 6:10–18; 1 Peter 5:6–11.

40

There are times when I am very focused upon my problems, so much so, that I totally miss what God is doing right in front of me. But the bottom line is this: whether I notice His hand at work in my life or not, He is there ... In the sunshine and in every storm of this life He is present for me and for all who believe in Him.

So much there is to thank You for in every situation

though often blessings lie beyond my means of comprehension.

Things I can't see and I can't know are hidden from my sight.

But later, I see clearly Your love, Your power, Your might

were working hard to help me move along my day's long road.

And all the while, Your angels here were helping with my load.

Dear Lord, You are the very best that *any friend* could be.

With all I am, I give You thanks for all You are to me!

With all my heart, I adore You—my very best Friend!

You have made known to me the path of life; you will fill me with joy in your presence, with eternal pleasures at your right hand.
—Psalm 16:11

See also: Psalms 119:33–40; 146:1–2; Micah 7:7; Zephaniah 3:17.

41

When I am going through a time of feeling sorry for myself for one reason or another, I can convince myself that no one gives a hoot about me ... that I am a loser in every respect of the word ... that I'm hardly worthy of the oxygen I take in. But when I go to God's Word and read a Psalm or a story that tells of His love for humanity, I am reminded that I am precious in His sight—and that is all I need. By opening myself up to Him, He is right on time with love, encouragement, grace, and mercy—while also bringing His peace and joy into my journey, exactly where I am, with exactly what I need.

When I am sad or angry, You seem so far away.

I wonder if You see me or hear me when I pray.

I wonder if You care at all. But then, truth comes to me:

I see You there upon the cross; in love You made me free.

So even though my tears may fall and sadness may close in,

when I open up Your Holy Word, You always help me win.

<blockquote>
With all my heart, I adore You—
the One who speaks love loud and clear!
</blockquote>

Do not be anxious about anything, but in everything, by prayer and petition, with thanksgiving, present your requests to God. And the peace of God which transcends all understanding will guard your hearts and your minds in Jesus Christ. Finally, brothers, whatever is true, whatever is right, whatever is pure, whatever is lovely, whatever is admirable – if anything is excellent or praiseworthy – think about such things.

Philippians 4:6-8

See also: Psalms 8; 16:11; 100; 119:105; 130:1–6; John 3:16–17; Romans 3:21–26; Ephesians 2:1–10; 1 Thessalonians 5:8–11.

42

God is the Rock—the most awesome, holy, and steady One, upon whom I can lean in all that life brings to me and all that I bring upon myself. In trouble and trial, in heartache and sadness, in any calamity, He is the One upon whom I can rely to rescue and save me from the ways of darkness. He holds me up. He leads me through—and out. He is the One who lovingly shows me the best way.

In the silence of my heartache, You whisper to be known,

speaking gently to my heart, and I know I'm not alone.

You are the One beside me, above me, and within.

You have no plan to leave me; You are closer than my skin.

Almighty God—the Father, Redeemer – Savior – Lord -

and precious Holy Spirit, through You, rich blessings poured.

With all my heart, I adore You—blessed Holy Trinity!

May the words of my mouth and the meditation of my heart be pleasing in your sight, O Lord, my Rock and my Redeemer.

—Psalm 19:14

See also: Psalm 31:1–3; James 1:2–4; 1 Peter 2:4–5.

43

When I seek God first—before my own agenda—there is peace. When I choose prayer as my first option—rather than my last resort—there is hope. And when I turn my focus first to trusting wholeheartedly in God's love for me—and away from all the things I can imagine could go wrong—there is joy.

When I trust You with my shattered dreams,
> I see You as my Friend.

You walk along beside me and guide me around each bend.

I see beauty in the ashes, when the fire subsides,

and remnants that are hidden not to be denied.

Below debris and brokenness, there lies a brand-new start,

and hope to find another dream for my trusting heart.

> With all my heart, I adore You—
> God who sees me, knows me, loves me!

You are my lamp, O LORD; the LORD turns my darkness into light.

—2 Samuel 22:29

See also: 2 Samuel 22:31–32; Psalm 91:14–16; 1 Peter 5:8–11.

44

My life is void of blessing when I live my hours in wishful thinking. But when I live my day in peaceful acceptance of what is, I am able to see blessing all around. No matter what I wish were different, if I will choose to accept what is ... if I am not in danger... and if I will keep my heart and my mind wide open for blessings, I will see them.

> So many times You've shown the way
>
> through heartaches—great and small;
>
> not even in a million years
>
> could I recount them all.
>
> From childhood into older years,
>
> Your faithfulness is true.
>
> Almighty God, my Dearest Friend,
>
> I bow to honor You!

With all my heart, I adore You—good and faithful Shepherd!

Better is one day in your courts than a thousand elsewhere; I would rather be a doorkeeper in the house of my God than dwell in the tents of the wicked.

—Psalm 84:10

See also: Psalms 23; 57:9–11; Lamentations 3:19–23; John 8:12; 10:14–15; 2 Corinthians 3:17–18.

45

Concerns and worries can make my life miserable —complicated—and very dark. Peace and light come in when I place my trust in God.

> To a world so much in need of hope,
>
> there's just one thing to say:
>
> There is a rock to lean upon
>
> that's sound in every way—
>
> Emmanuel, the Father's Son;
>
> Redeemer—Savior—King—
>
> Messiah promised for all time,
>
> peace, hope, and joy You bring!

With all my heart, I adore You—holy Promised One!

For to us a child is born, to us a son is given, and the government will be on his shoulders. And he will be called Wonderful Counselor, Mighty God, Everlasting Father, Prince of Peace.
—Isaiah 9:6

See also: Psalms 18:1–3; 63:7–8; Matthew 7:24–27; Galatians 2:20–21; 2 Timothy 2:11–13.

46

Trouble, problems, heartaches, calamities, and all such things are temporary events in this life. And though I may view these things as stuff I just need to "get through" on my own, God did not create me with the ability nor the desire to travel through such times as these on my own. He offers me His faithfulness and His people to help and encourage me.

> Though I'm tempted just to carry all my burdens and my care,
>
> I know that's not Your plan: arms outstretched and waiting there . . .
>
> saying, "Take My yoke upon you; it is lighter than your load."
>
> So I give You what I carry as we walk along life's road.
>
> And the moment that I do so, it's as clear as it can be:
>
> that You are sure the dearest Friend that anyone could be!
>
>> With all my heart, I adore You—God who loves me dearly through Yourself and others!

"Come to me, all you who are weary and burdened, and I will give you rest. Take my yoke upon you and learn from me, for I am gentle and humble in heart, and you will find rest for your souls."
—Matthew 11:28–29

See also: Psalms 23:4; 34:18; 90:1–2; Proverbs 17:17; Ecclesiastes 4:9–12; John 14:1, 15–27; 1 John 4:21.

47

I can remember a period of intense fear as if it happened yesterday. The energy I felt in response to the fear seemed not my own, but coming from a source deep within. It reminded me of a continual gust of powerful wind, energizing me to complete the necessary tasks of moving away from the danger. And though in the end, sorrow washed over me like a heavy downfall of rain, I also remember the feeling of safety and peace. I had been delivered. And there was a knowing that something better—beyond all that I had just experienced—was yet to be.

>Pour me out, Lord. Use me.
>
>Complete Your will Your way.
>
>No matter what my fear may be,
>
>grant me words to say.
>
>And give my heart the courage
>
>to speak Your name aloud
>
>to any who are troubled
>
>or threatened by the proud.

With all my heart, I adore You—divine Deliverer!

*He gives strength to the weary and increases the power of the weak. Even youths grow tired and weary, and young men stumble and fall; but those who hope in the L*ord *will renew their strength. They will soar on wings like eagles; they will run and not grow weary, they will walk and not be faint.*

—Isaiah 40:29–31

See also: Psalms 34:4; 46:1–3; 118:28–29; Habakkuk 3:19; Ephesians 6:10–18.

48

It is important to regularly check the foundation upon which I am building and living my life. I learned the value of this practice many years ago while living in an old farmhouse. If a crack shows up in the foundation, it is a very good indication that a shift has taken place, and big trouble may be brewing. Action is needed—perhaps quickly—to prevent further damages.

Upon what am I building life? Is it a solid plan?

Or is it just a patched-up thing from the mind of man?

Am I building on the Rock: the One and True Foundation

that does not change or shift about by manipulation?

Am I grounded in God's Word or my own strategy,

which keeps my life a wobbly thing where I just worship me?

With all my heart, I adore You—he One who helps me see Truth!

> *"Therefore everyone who hears these words of mine and puts them into practice is like a wise man who built his house on the rock. The rain came down, the streams rose, and the winds blew and beat against that house; yet it did not fall, because it had its foundation on the rock."*
>
> —Matthew 7:24–25

See also: Isaiah 28:16; 1 Corinthians 3:18–20; Ephesians 2:17–22; 2 Timothy 2:19.

49

Because of God's great love, I can experience resurrection in death, joy in sorrow, peace in pain. It is God's Holy Spirit who brings life and hope into places where none seems to be found. I can be confident that as He walked with Moses in Bible times and all others who have trusted Him throughout history, He does now—and always will—walk with me.

> The thought of Your mercy
>
> brings joy to my soul.
>
> Though I see myself broken,
>
> You see me as whole.
>
> And through Your intention,
>
> compassion, and love,
>
> You come to redeem me
>
> from Your throne above.

With all my heart, I adore You—precious Savior!

In him our hearts rejoice, for we trust in his holy name.

—Psalm 33:21

See also: Psalms 29; 31; 86:11–13; John 3:16–17.

50

I can face today, tomorrow, and every day thereafter with confidence because God has proven He is trustworthy. And because I am aware that His Holy Spirit lives within me through my faith in Jesus as Savior and Friend, I can take each step of my earthly journey with hope, knowing that no matter what may come into or go out of my life, I am known, loved, treasured, and cherished by the One who created me and redeems my life daily.

> God of old and God of new,
>
> that's who You are. That is You . . .
>
> moving forward every day,
>
> bringing Self in Your own way.
>
> New generations will arise . . .
>
> they'll be in Your loving eyes.
>
> And so will I, as older, be
>
> loved by You, who's watching me.
>
> With all my heart, I adore You—
> Wonderful Counselor, Everlasting Father, Prince of Peace!

Lord, you have been our dwelling place throughout all generations. Before the mountains were born or you brought forth the earth and the world, from everlasting to everlasting you are God.

—Psalm 90:1–2

See also: Psalms 31:15–16; 56:8; 102; 145; Proverbs 3:5–8; Isaiah 9:2–7; 43:18–19; Romans 8:1–17; Hebrews 12:1–3; 1 Peter 4:7–11.

51

When Jesus knew that His betrayal, arrest, trial, and crucifixion were drawing near, He prayed for Himself, His followers, and all who would ever believe in Him. He spent time with His disciples, explaining the things that were to take place. He promised them that His Father would be sending the Holy Spirit to comfort and guide them when He would no longer be physically present with them. In overwhelming sorrow, He went to the Garden of Gethsemane with a few of His beloved disciples—men with whom He had traveled, taught, and performed many miracles. He asked them to stay alert, keep watch, and pray. The gospels record that He then left them and walked alone to His favorite place in the Garden. There He prayed, and He wept . . . "his sweat was like drops of blood falling to the ground" (Luke 22:44). Two times, Jesus checked on the disciples and found them sleeping. He woke them up and returned to prayer. The third time He found them asleep, He woke them again and said, "Rise! Let us go! Here comes my betrayer" (Mark 14:42). Jesus did not condemn His followers for sleeping; He knew they were exhausted, and He accepted their humanity. Even in His sorrow, He loved them as He had from the beginning.

No wonder I adore Him!

Unwavering love and faithfulness are gifts You offer all;

though some will doubt and turn away, You never cease to call.

The same today and yesterday and in all years to be

faithful Savior . . dearest Friend . . one Holy Trinity!

With all my heart, I adore You, O Lord!

He is the image of the invisible God, the firstborn over all creation. For by him all things were created: things in heaven and on earth, visible and invisible, whether thrones or powers or rulers or authorities; all things were created by him and for him. He is before all things, and in him all things hold together. And he is the head of the body, the church; he is the beginning and the firstborn from among the dead, so that in everything he might have the supremacy. For God was pleased to have all his fullness dwell in him, and through him to reconcile to himself all things, whether things on earth or things in heaven, by making peace through his blood, shed on the cross.

—Colossians 1:15–20

See also: Psalms 117; 139:1–18; John 3:16–21; Colossians 1:21–29; Hebrews 13:8.

52

While Jesus lived on the earth and traveled with His disciples to tell of God's love, mercy, and plan of salvation for all humanity, He challenged and upset many very intelligent people who saw Him as a troublemaker, a heretic, or even a crazy man.

Nicodemus, Israel's teacher and a member of the Jewish ruling council, went secretly at night to ask important questions of Jesus. These are the words of Jesus in response, as He explained eternal life—and His own part in it—to this very important man:

> *"Just as Moses lifted up the snake in the desert, so the Son of Man must be lifted up, that everyone who believes in him may have eternal life. For God so loved the world that he gave his one and only Son, that whoever believes in him shall not perish but have eternal life. For God did not send his Son into the world to condemn the world, but to save the world through him. Whoever believes in him is not condemned, but whoever does not believe stands condemned already because he has not believed in the name of God's one and only Son."*
>
> —John 3:14–18

Though Your truth has been told time and again,

still there are doubters - plenty of them.

I just don't get it; I cannot see why

One so beloved and willing to die

would be ridiculed, scorned, and mocked in the face

while Your whole agenda was to offer God's grace.

Yet . . .I've had *my* doubts. I can clearly see *me*

as one needing mercy and pardon from Thee.

With all my heart, I adore You – precious Savior, dearest Friend!

> *But he was pierced for our transgressions, he was crushed for our iniquities; the punishment that brought us peace was upon him, and by his wounds we are healed.*
>
> —Isaiah 53:5

See also: Matthew 26:36-46; Mark 14:32-42; Luke 22:39-46; John 13:1-17;14;17:6-26

53

While walking through a garden nursery recently, I noticed a plaque on the wall with these words: "Your mind is a garden. Your thoughts are the seeds. You can grow flowers. Or you can grow weeds." (author unknown).

Since reading them, I have contemplated those words many times. And they come to mind again as I conclude this book.

I have noticed many blessings in my life that have come forward since making and taking the time for intentional daily Bible reading. When I do my part to plant God's Word into my mind, He blesses. Abundantly.

I stay ready to see blossoms in every single day

when I invite Your Holy Word to come; to guide; to stay.

With all I am I praise You – sweet Holy Trinity

for all You are and have been; for all You'll ever be.

You've proven to me many times that I can count on You:

Creator – Savior – Spirit – so TRUSTWORTHY AND TRUE!

> *Trust in the Lord with all your heart and lean not on your own understanding; in all your ways acknowledge him, and he will make your paths straight. Do not be wise in your own eyes; fear the Lord and shun evil. This will bring health to your body and nourishment to your bones.*
>
> —Proverbs 3:5-8

Endnote

1. Oswald Chambers, *My Utmost for His Highest*, February 22.

About the Author

Now in the seventh decade of my life, I cannot remember a time when I have not loved to write. When my three children were young, I wrote poems, articles, and stories for religious publications and a small weekly newspaper. In 1984, it was a sweet surprise to be invited to publish a children's book through Concordia Publishing House of Missouri. I had sent a poem to them, hoping it would be included in a poetry book for children, but the editor saw its possibility as a book and lined me up with a very talented illustrator. *Jesus Is My Very Best Friend* sold well for many years, though it is no longer in print. My name at that time was Barbara A Young, and the book illustrator was Kathy Mitter. Though I am not at all a Bible scholar, I have loved God's Holy Word since I was very young. The miracles and wonders of creation invited me to know and love our Creator God as a small child. The Old Testament stories of people like Noah, Job, and Ruth helped me better understand that God has many emotions and carefully watches over those who follow His ways. He is loving and merciful, as well as sometimes angry and jealous for His own good reasons. As He commands us, He is so worthy of respect and honor. The New Testament accounts of the life, death, and resurrection of Jesus, along with the stories of those who lived at the same time and knew my Savior as a personal Guide and Friend, along with those who were anointed by His Holy Spirit, certainly inspire and encourage me in my walk of faith today. It would be difficult to choose my favorite books of the Bible, but the Psalms are among them . . . which is why you will find many references to the Psalms as you read through this book. I hope that you will enjoy the poetry prayers. I chose to write in first person, because I can only speak for myself, but I hope you will find a few that also speak for you. I was born, was raised, and continue to reside in the state of Ohio—now living near Columbus. Besides reading and writing, I love spending time with family and friends; watching wholesome movies about real people; taking road trips; any opportunities to interact and serve with others through my church, community, and the KAIROS prison ministry; as well as a good cup of coffee and a piece of milk chocolate. Christmas is my favorite holiday—with a little bit of Santa and a whole lot of Jesus. Whoever you are, I have been praying for you since this book was first imagined. May you continue to seek out the knowledge, wisdom, and love of the Holy Trinity. In so doing, I am confident that you will be blessed . . . abundantly.

www.ingramcontent.com/pod-product-compliance
Lightning Source LLC
Chambersburg PA
CBHW072133070526
44585CB00016B/1659